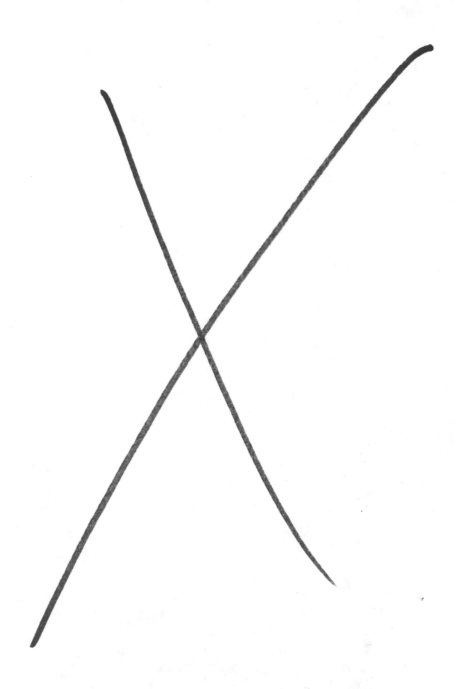

Caps, Hats, Socks, AND Mittens

A Book About the Four Seasons

by LOUISE BORDEN

illustrated by LILLIAN HOBAN

SCHOLASTIC INC.

New York Toronto London Auckland Sydney

ISBN 0-590-44872-2

Text copyright © 1989 by Louise W. Borden.
Illustrations copyright © 1989 by Lillian Hoban.
All rights reserved. Published by Scholastic Inc.
BLUE RIBBON is a registered trademark of Scholastic Inc.

15   9/9 0 1 2/0

Printed in the U.S.A.   23

For Catie and Ayars
—L.B.

Winter is
caps,
hats,
socks,
and mittens.

Winter is
red sleds
up
a
hill.

Winter is
red sleds
down
a
hill.

Winter is
a lot of stuff to put on
and a lot of stuff
to get off!

Winter is fun
out and in.

Winter is
hot mugs
and hot cups.
Yum, yum.

Winter is
snug in bed.

Spring is
grass, grass, grass.
Dad cuts the grass
and cuts the grass
and cuts the grass.

Spring is mud to dig.
Mud on my hands.
Mud on my pants.
Mud in my pan.
Mud in my can.
A mud song!

Spring is
pots and plants
and plants in pots.

Spring is a nest of eggs,
a bed of twigs
and grass
and moss.

Spring is wet.
Drip, drip, drip.
Drip, drip, drip.

Spring is
picnics
in the sun.

Spring is
run, run, run!
Up, up, up!

Summer is
sun and sand,
flags and bands.

Summer is hot, hot, hot.
Lots of hot dogs.
Hot dog and hot dogs.

Summer is a ball game.
"I can bat."
"I can toss."
Caps off!
Hats off!
"I lost my mitt!"

Summer is . . .
"I can swim!"
"I can swim fast."
"1 . . . 2 . . . 3 . . ."
"Jump!"

Summer is
a jar full of bugs.

Summer is a fish in a pond
and a frog on a pad.

Fall is lots of smells.
Nuts and pumpkins
and corn in husks.

Fall is
red,
orange,
yellow,
brown
at dusk.

Fall is
pens and desks.

Last on the bus!
First off the bus!

Fall is
frost on the grass
before the sun is up.

Fall is soccer.
Soccer is fun.
We run.
We kick.
"Hands off the ball!"

Fall is black cats
and black hats
after the sun is down.

Then back to . . .
caps,
hats,
socks,
and mittens.